AF605097

BEACHES

BEACHES

AUSTRALIAN COASTLINES

INTRODUCTION

Australian beaches are renowned for their stunning beauty and diverse landscapes.

From the golden sands of Bondi Beach to the rugged cliffs of the Great Ocean Road, each beach offers its own unique charm. The crystal-clear waters invite swimmers and surfers alike, while the vibrant marine life beneath the waves calls to snorkellers and divers.

Whether you're seeking the bustling atmosphere of a popular tourist spot or the tranquillity of a secluded cove, Australian beaches provide the perfect backdrop for relaxation and adventure.

As the sun sets, painting the sky in hues of orange and pink, there's no better place to reflect on the natural wonders of this magnificent country.

The gentle sound of waves kissing the shore lulls you into a state of serene

Point Addis, Victoria.

bliss, as a cool breeze carries the scent of salt and freedom. Families gather for picnics, children giggle as they build sandcastles, and couples stroll hand in hand, leaving footprints that the tide will soon erase.

Lifeguards keep a watchful eye, ensuring safety amidst the playful chaos, while skilled surfers carve through the waves with grace and agility.

For those who love to explore, walking trails wind through coastal dunes and lush vegetation, revealing breathtaking vistas at every turn. You might even stumble upon hidden rock pools, teeming with colourful sea creatures, or spot dolphins playfully leaping in the distance.

Local cafés and beachfront eateries offer a taste of fresh seafood and refreshing drinks, allowing you to savour the culinary delights of the coast as the day winds down. In the evenings, beachside bonfires crackle and glow, drawing people together to share stories and laughter under a canopy of stars.

Australian beaches are more than just a destination; they are a quintessential part of the country's soul, offering endless opportunities to connect with nature, find peace, and create cherished memories.

Ocean swimming pools are located at some beaches across Australia and where locals and visitors can swim in a unique experience that combines the thrill of open water with the safety and structure of a pool. The gentle rhythm of the waves provides a natural resistance that can make your swim both challenging and invigorating.

The rockpools you will find at some beaches in Australia have a treasure trove of marine life waiting to be discovered. These natural formations are like miniature aquariums, with tiny fish darting about in shallow waters. Exploring rockpools is not just a visual treat but also an educational experience, offering a glimpse into the delicate ecosystems that thrive along Australia's vast coastline. There are many hidden gems of amazing rockpools for nature lovers and are unique to the beach or coastline in that state.

At dusk and when the sun is going down, watching an Australian sunset on the beach full of breathtaking colours of orange, purple and pinks from the golden sands there is no doubt that the Australian coastlines and beaches are truly one of the most beautiful environments to experience pure serenity bathed in beauty and peace.

Anna Bay, near Newcastle.

NEW SOUTH WALES

Merimbula, far South Coast, NSW.

Hyams Beach, NSW.

Jervis Bay, NSW.

Thirroul Beach, NSW.

SYDNEY

High tide at Cronulla Beach, Sydney.

Maroubra Beach, Sydney.

Bondi Beach.

SYDNEY'S ICONIC BONDI BEACH

Located just seven kilometers from Sydney's Central Business District, Bondi Beach is not only one of the most renowned and famous beaches in the world but is also the backdrop for popular TV shows such as *Bondi Rescue* and *Bondi Vet*.

The Historic Swimming Club was founded in 1929, and the Bondi Icebergs Swimming Club welcomes the public to experience its rich history, and above it, you'll find the delightful Icebergs Dining Room and Bar.

Aside from the bars and restaurants nearby, most locals like to do the Bondi to Coogee Coastal Walk which offers a stunning six-kilometre trail featuring breathtaking views of the ocean.

Additionally, during the summer months, the coastline showcases the largest outdoor sculpture exhibition, Sculpture by the Sea.

The City to Surf is the largest running event in the world, which is held each year in August. The race attracts over 80,000 entrants who complete the 14 km run or walk from the Sydney central business district to the beach.

This iconic beach is a slice of heaven from morning to evening.

Bondi Icebergs Swimming Pool at Bondi Beach.

Icebergs Bondi Beach.

Overview of Bondi Beach, Sydney.

Bronte Beach, near Bondi Beach, Sydney.

LIFEGUARD

Balmoral Beach, Mosman, Sydney, including the famous Bathers' Pavilion.

Shelly Beach, Manly, Sydney.

Manly Beach, Sydney.

One of Sydney's most famous beaches, Manly Beach.

Overview of Manly, Sydney.

Dee Why, Sydney.

Palm Beach, Sydney.

Palm Beach, Sydney.

Pearl Beach, Central Coast, NSW.

The Entrance, Central Coast, NSW.

Avoca Beach, NSW.

Caves Beach, NSW.

Newcastle has stunning beaches and a number of historic sites.

Port Stephens, NSW.

Port Macquarie, NSW.

Blueys Beach, NSW.

Coffs Harbour, NSW.

Ballina, NSW.

Lennox Heads, NSW.

Byron Bay, NSW.

BYRON BAY

BYRON BAY

Byron Bay is a coastal town in New South Wales.

Cape Byron, the eastern most point of Australia, is home to the iconic Cape Byron Lighthouse, built in 1901.

Longboard surfers arrived in the 1960s to surf some of the best waves in Australia.

The laid back and creative community with an innovative food scene makes Byron a great destination for tourists.

With nature on the doorstep of Byron, incredible sunrises and local fresh produce served at the many restaurants and bars it is a people watching seaside town.

Cape Byron Lighthouse.

QUEENSLAND

Burleigh Heads, Queensland.

Burleigh Heads, Queensland.

Gold Coast, Queensland.

Gold Coast, Queensland.

Gold Coast, Queensland.

Surfers Paradise, Gold Coast.

Main Beach, Queensland.

Noosa, Queensland.

Double Island Beach, Queensland.

Bribie Island, Queensland.

Kings Beach, Caloundra, Queensland.

Trinity Beach, Queensland.

Trinity Beach, Queensland.

Torquay Beach,Hervey Bay, Queensland.

Yeppoon, Queensland.

Green Island, Cairns, North Queensland

Palm Cove, Queensland.

Port Douglas,Queensland.

Balanced rock stacks line the shoreline on Captain Cook Highway, Far North Queensland.

Rock stacks, Captain Cook Highway.

White Heaven Beach, Queensland.

White Heaven Beach, Queensland.

Hamilton Island, Queensland.

Great Keppel Island, Queensland.

Dunk Island, Queensland.

Hook Island, Queensland.

Magnetic Island Beach, Queensland.

Remote beachscape in the Daintree at Far North Queensland.

Myall Beach, Cape Tribulation, Far North Queensland.

Cape Hillsborough, National Park, Queensland.

NORTHERN TERRITORY

Darwin City Beach.

Darwin, Northern Territory.

Mindil Beach, Darwin, Northern Territory.

Mindil Beach, Darwin, Northern Territory.

Nightcliff Beach, Darwin, Northern Territory.

Mindil Beach, Darwin, Northern Territory.

Mindil Beach, Darwin, Northern Territory.

Casuarina Coastal Reserve, Northern Territory.

East Woody Beach, an iconic tourist popular place in Nhulunby, a township on the Gove Peninsula, Northern Territory.

Five Mile Beach, Northern Territory.

Dundee Beach, Northern Territory.

Dundee Beach in the Northern Territory.

Lee Point Beach at low tide. Lee Point is north of the city of Darwin.

Bathurst Island, one of the Tiwi Islands of the Northern Territory.

Top End creek and beach.

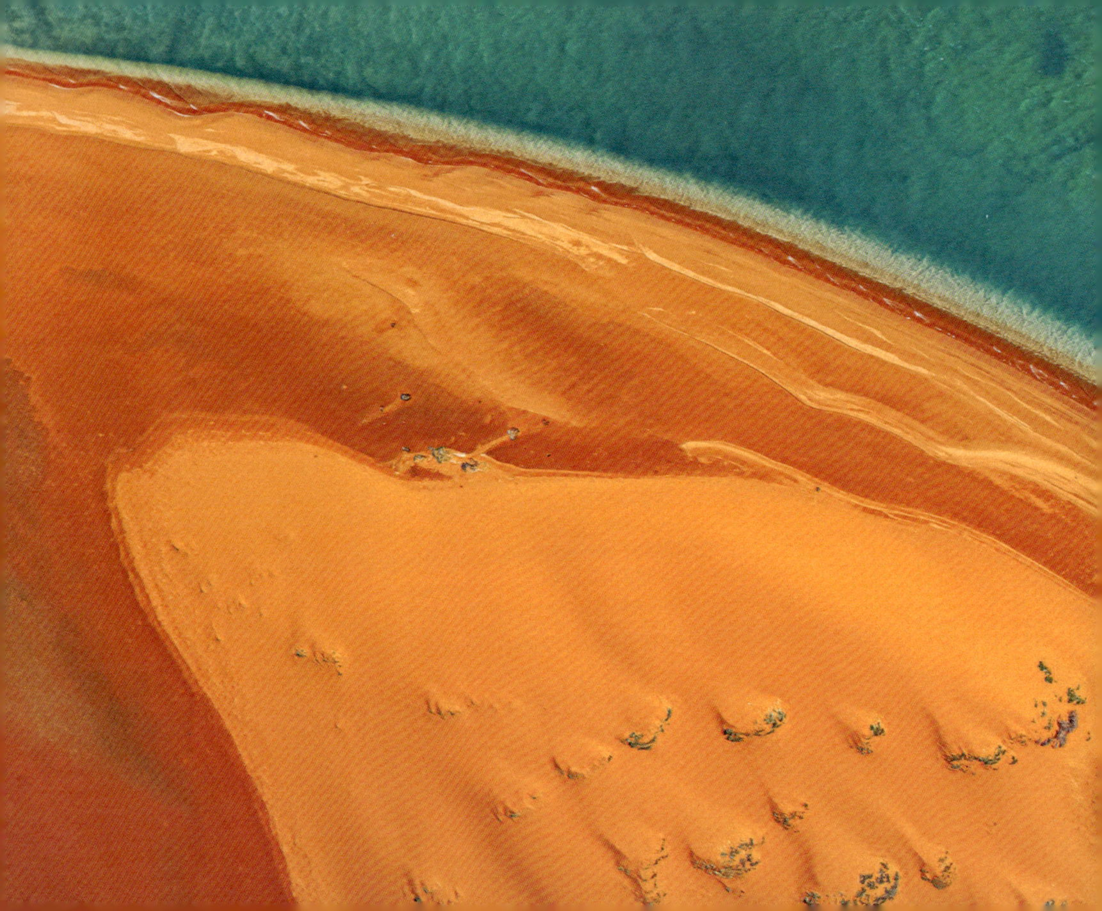

WESTERN AUSTRALIA

Cape Leveque, Dampier Peninsula, Western Australia.

Sunset at Cape Leveque in the north west of Western Australia.

Broome, a coastal town in the Kimberley region of Western Australia.

Cable Beach, Broome, Western Australia.

Cable Beach, Broome, Western Australia.

Red Sand Beach, Roebuck Bay, Broome, Western Australia.

Eighty Mile Beach, located on the beachfront between Port Hedland and Broom Australia.

Eighty Mile Beach, Western Australia.

Eighty Mile Beach, Western Australia.

The coast of Cape Keraudren, a remote area between Port Hedland and Broome in Western Australia.

Hearson Cove in the Pilbra, Western Australia.

Point Samson, on the remote Pilbara coast of Western Australia.

Beach and boulders at the remote Hearson Cove, Burrup Peninsula, Karratha, Western Australia.

Karratha, Western Australia.

Cape Beach, Western Australia.

Cape Leveque, Western Australia.

Cape Range National Park

Wildlife in Exmouth, Ningaloo, Western Australia.

Whale shark swimming on the Ningaloo Reef, Western Australia.

Exmouth, Western Australia

Cape Range National Park, Ningaloo Reef, near Exmouth, Western Australia.

Cape Range National Park near Exmouth, Western Australia.

The Ningaloo Reef and Beach, Western Australia.

Dolphins in Monkey Mia, Western Australia.

Wild emu family at Shark Bay, Western Australia.

Geraldton, Western Australia.

Geraldton, Western Australia.

Hutt Lagoon, Pink Lake, Western Australia.

Coogee Beach and the *Omeo* shipwreck in Fremantle, Western Australia.

Rottnest Island, Western Australia.

Bathers Beach in Fremantle, Western Australia.

Cottesloe Beach, Western Australia.

Cottesloe Beach, Western Australia.

Perth Beach, Western Australia.

Rockingham foreshore with a jetty in Perth, Western Australia.

Penguins at Penguin Island, Rockingham, Western Australia.

Busselton Jetty, Western Australia.

Little Beach in Albany, Western Australia.

Wild Sea Lion which comes ashore every day in Esperance, Western Australia.

Kangaroo family on the beach of Lucky Bay, Esperance, Western Australia.

Lucky Bay in Esperance, Western Australia.

Misery Beach, Albany, Western Australia.

Cape Arid, Western Australia.

SOUTH AUSTRALIA

Eucla, Western Australia and South Australia border.

Marion Bay Coast, South Australia.

Coffin Bay National Park, South Australia.

Coffin Bay, South Australia.

Eyre Peninsula, South Australia.

Eyre Peninsula, South Australia.

Kangaroo Island, South Australia.

Hanson Bay on Kangaroo Island, South Australia.

Kangaroo Island, South Australia.

Kangaroo Island, Pennington Bay, South Australia.

Stokes Bay Beach, Kangaroo Island, South Australia.

Stokes Bay Beach, Kangaroo Island, South Australia.

Rapid Bay, South Australia.

Aldinga Beach, Southern Adelaide.

West Beach, Adelaide shores, South Australia.

Sellicks Beach, South Australia.

Glenelg Beach, South Australia.

Southport Beach, South Australia.

VICTORIA

Portland, Victoria.

Warrnambool, Victoria.

Coastline Warrnambool, Victoria.

Point Ritchie Lookout in Warrnambool, Victoria.

The Twelve Apostles, Great Ocean Road, Victoria.

Great Ocean Road, Loch Ard Gorge, Port Campbell National Park, Victoria.

Loch Ard Gorge, Port Campbell National Park, Victoria.

Twelve Apostles, Great Ocean Road, Victoria.

Great Ocean Road, Victoria.

Apollo Bay, Victoria.

Apollo Bay, Victoria.

Anglesea township and Point Roadknight headland, Great Ocean Road, Victoria.

Bells Beach, Victoria.

Bells Beach, Torquay, Victoria.

Bells Beach, Torquay, Victoria.

Bells Beach, Victoria.

Lorne, Victoria.

Geelong Waterfront, Victoria.

Barwon Heads.

Point Lonsdale Pier.

The Point Lonsdale Lighthouse.

Point Lonsdale, Victoria.

St Leonards, on the Bellarine Peninsula in Victoria.

St Kilda Beach, Melbourne.

Brighton Bay Beachhouses, Victoria.

Frankston, Victoria.

Phillip Island, Victoria.

Phillip Island, Victoria.

Woolamai Beach, Phillip Island, Victoria.

TASMANIA

Bruny Island, Tasmania.

South Cape Bay, Tasmania.

Bay of Fires, Tasmania.

Bay of Fires, Tasmania.

Bay of Fires, Tasmania.

The Nut, Stanley, Tasmania.

Binalong Bay, Tasmania.

Binalong Bay, Tasmania.

Wineglass Bay, Tasmania.

Flinders Island, Tasmania.

Hazards Beach, Tasmania.

Honeymoon Bay, Freycinet Peninsula.

Wineglass Bay, Freycinet National Park.

Kingston Beach in Hobart.

Opossum Bay, Hobart.

Seven Miles Beach, Tasmania.

Sawyer Bay, Tasmania.

Sawyer Bay, Tasmania.

Denison Beach and the A3 Tasman Highway, Tasmania.

SUNSETS & SUNRISES

Southport, South Australia.

Palm Beach, Sydney.

Esperance, Western Australia.

Sorrento, Victoria.

Bondi Beach, Sydney.

Eaglehawk Neck, Tasmania.

Coffin Bay, South Australia.

Broome, Western Australia.

Noosa, Queensland.

Gold Coast, Queensland.

First published in 2026 by New Holland Publishers

newhollandpublishers.com

Copyright © 2026 New Holland Publishers
Copyright © 2026 in images: New Holland Image Library, Shutterstock or Adobe Stock.

All rights reserved. No part of this publication may be reproduced, stored in a retrieval system or transmitted, in any form or by any means, electronic, mechanical, photocopying, recording or otherwise, without the prior written permission of the publishers and copyright holders.

A record of this book is held at the National Library of Australia.

ISBN 9781760798505

Managing Director: Fiona Schultz
General Manager/Publisher: Olga Dementiev
Designer: Andrew Davies
Production Director: Arlene Gippert

Keep up with New Holland Publishers:

NewHollandPublishers
@newhollandpublishers

BEACH